To Gordon
God bless [illegible]
always. Jesus loves you and
has great things for you all!!

Fishin'

A Poetry Collection

Love

Lorn Johnson

250-467-3954

Fishin'

A Poetry Collection

by Lorn Johnson

Johnson, Lorn

FISHIN'
A Poetry Collection.

Published by: Lorn Johnson, Dawson Creek, B.C.

ISBN 978-1-927588-26-0

Publication assistance and digital printing in Canada by

PageMaster PUBLICATION SERVICES INC.
www.pagemaster.ca

Preface

Please understand Jesus gave the words to be written down. They were gathered from going to meetings, praising God, reading the Word and getting in the Spirit. I get so much by watching people singing songs, giving testimonies, the preaching of the word, but the most precious thing of all is to see people give their hearts to the Lord.

I went to a meeting one night and went up for prayer. I asked the Lord to clean out my vessel and most of all fill it up with good. I went home and had a sleep and when I got up I started getting lines and verses in my head. I could hardly write them down as fast as they came, I wrote for about 14 hours (wrote 3 new pens out of ink), had a sleep and wrote for about another 14 or 15 hours. It was like the Lord was sitting right beside me. One of the first things the Lord said was that all of this was not just for me, that it was for everyone else. I give all the glory and honour to my Lord and Saviour Jesus Christ.

P.S. Thank you all for the all the words and the strength to write them down and for putting things in place for this book.

Amen

Lorn

FISHIN'

The Lord took me out fishin'
Just the other day
We did not go to the same old hole
For we went a different way

Now come to think of it
We took no hooks or line
We did not take any rods at all
But we made out just fine

I don't know if you know the story
About the fishers of men
You do not need a licence
And you can catch as many as you can

Sometimes you can fish for days
And you will not catch a thing
But when Jesus says put your net down
It's like they are jumping in

So let's put our faith in Jesus
He is the Master of all seas
He knows when the fish are biting
And just where they will be

There are always more fish out there
But you need to seek to find
And we can catch them with the Word
Instead of hooks and line

THE WORDS

I don't know the words Lord
Please tell me so I can write them down
So I can share them with others, Lord
And tell of what I found

Please let these words
Be the kindest they will ever hear
Let them bring love, joy and peace
And dry up every tear

Let them be an inspiration
To everyone I meet
Let them give back hope that was lost
And put people back on their feet

Let the living word
Break the chains and set free
Just do for them dear Lord
What You have done for me

So let us all repent
Stop doing and change our ways
And seek the Lord's face daily
Like the Bible says

The Lord is always there
And this I know is true
You see all these words were given
As encouragement to you

MUSIC MAKER

Thank you Lord
For playing guitar for me
And all the other instruments
To form a symphony

To make it sound glorious
As only you can do
Putting loving kindness in there
Hope and inspiration too

Sending the Holy Ghost
To each and every one
Coming from the Father
At the promise of the Son

Let the music play
Like none have ever heard
Let it be almighty
With the preaching of the Word

Let it reach all people
As only You can do
Like a little baby crying
And looking up at you

Can you hear Jesus, people
He is calling out your name
We cannot all play guitar
But Jesus loves all the same

CLOSER WE GET

Lord we only get closer
Each day you give me more
You're my hope for all tomorrows
And what they hold in store

My cup is running over
For You have given, oh so much
With your loving kindness
And the grace of your touch

Jesus I just love You
More I cannot say
And thank You for loving me
And helping me find my way

Thank You Lord
For all the things You have done
All the things You are doing
And all those yet to come

You make me whole again
Which makes me complete
Not captive to anything
When I am kneeling at Your feet

Thank You Holy One
For keeping me on track
And may I just glorify Your name
By just loving You right back

CHANGE

Some years ago I would use
The Lord's name in vain
Now I simply praise it
My, how people say I've changed

When you are stuck in the world
There is not much you won't do
Because when it comes right down to it
You are glorifying you

We think we can make it
Just simply on our own
That we are ten feet tall and bulletproof
And the world is our throne

We can go through all our life
With this concept in our mind
But we are walking in darkness
Lost and hurt ,but mostly just blind

We cannot see past our pride
Until we kneel before our God
And humble ourselves as little children
To some this may be quite odd

But if all you know is the world
It can be hard to let it go
Just cry out to Jesus
He is there for everyone you know

You may even change
I mean just look at me
I was stuck in the world once
But Jesus set me free

SWEETER

I heard things just get sweeter
As we all go on through time
If we know our Lord and Saviour
And let that Jesus light shine

Just let people see Jesus
In everything you do
No matter where you are
Because Jesus lives in you

Let us learn to be humble
And fall down on our knees
Open up the most holy of doors
By simply saying please

Please dear Lord it's me again
Can you listen to my call
You are faithful and forgiving
And there for one and all

You are the risen King
The One who conquered the grave
The One who gave His life
So the world could be saved

There is no greater love
Than what You did for me
I see this now with willing eyes
And pray it will always be

So sweet is every moment
That I get to spend with You
You are that shining light
And You always do come through

A TIME IS COMING

There is a time coming in the future
When we will all seek the Lord's face
It will not matter who you are
There will come a time and a place

Where this world won't matter
And the things of it are gone
It's like the setting of the sun
And its rise again at dawn

Things that happen everyday
Will simply be no more
The past will be gone forever
A new kingdom is in store

When all the chains of this world
Will simply be undone
And the One we have to answer to
Is Jesus Christ the Son

The One who gave His life
So that everyone else could live
How much more do we want
Jesus gave all He could give

So we need to praise Jesus
And ask all in His holy name
To pray that we are worthy
And know He took the blame

Jesus came and died for us
So it is not too much to do
Let's give Him all the glory
And simply say, thank you

YOU LEAD

Lord You woke me up this morning
I don't know what to say
So I am asking for your help
Would You please lead the way

I want You to go before me
Just making clear the way
You lead and I will follow
For this I have to pray

I pray I do Your will Lord
And not a bit of mine
That I pick my cross up daily
And let Your glory shine

For You give me more each day
Than I can take all in
And for that dear Lord
I say thank you, simply once again

I know You will be there
In everything I do
I pray people don't see me at all
But Jesus shining through

So thank you for the early start
And all the help along the way
As I look out my window
And know You made this day

This has been a special time
Just sharing this with you
It really meant a lot to me
I hope it did for you

WEATHER CHANGE

I woke up one morning very thankful
Knowing God is awesome in all ways
Yesterday He brought warm weather
And He brought it out again today

You see I had to work outside
And it had been kind of cold
My back was sore and my knees hurt
I guess I am getting old

Now my Father up above
Must have been looking down
And showed His mercy on me
Knowing it hurt to get around

What a kind and loving God
To be so nice to me
I really must say thank you
Down on bended knees

Just to know He is watching over me
And cares so very much
To know He can change the weather
With His awesome touch

So get to know the Lord
He wants to do things for you
And one day when it is cold outside
He might warm it up for you

LORD KNOWS

The Lord told me to slow down
I was going way too fast
Just to sit and be still
There is a storm coming that has to pass

The Lord knows what's coming
And what it holds for you
So you better listen up
And be careful what you do

Don't take things for granted
They are never that way
Just like humbling yourself
When you take time to pray

To get down on bended knees
Even when they hurt
To make the extra effort
For everything it's worth

To talk to our Lord and Saviour
To have that one-on-one
A simple showing of respect
For things already done

So please dear people
Listen to what I say
The Lord is more than worthy
Of our honour and our praise

So respect your Holy time
With the One who is Most High
Just give Him all the glory
And never question why

SHARE THAT LIVING WATER

When you find that living water
Keep going back for more
And keep sharing it with others
That's what it's really for

To give hope to someone
Who is simply feeling down
To share the word that you have heard
With everyone around

To laugh and cry together
In the body, all as one
Knowing that salvation comes
Only through the Son

So lay it at Jesus' feet
And nail it to the cross
Because it all died with Him that day
Through the life that it cost

You don't have to worry
It never will run out
Just flood the world with the Word
For that's what it's all about

So just let that living water
Be an overflowing well
And teach people how to pray
And be born again as well

DEAD MEETINGS

Now I have been going to meetings
For a little while
They all have been different
Each one has its style

Some that you go to
The meeting starts out dead
It's like you're at the morgue
And your eulogy's been read

But you never know what will happen
When you clean out your heart
A meeting that starts out dead
Is alive again, when we all do our part

And when the Holy Spirit comes
Because He has been invited in
Nothing can hold you back
And you can only win

I have seen people healed
And other people saved
When we all do our part
By this I mean we prayed

Some sing songs
The most beautiful I've ever heard
And others give us scripture
And fill us with the Word

Some are there to testify
About something that has happened to them
Or maybe someone else, a family member
Or simply just a friend

I have seen a preacher
Whose fire had gone out
And the next time I saw Him
A powerful sermon came out

So if you think the Lord
Cannot do much for you
Just give up your will to Him
And see what He can do

For Jesus can do anything
That is very plain to see
Just think of all the words you just heard
It was Jesus talking and simply using me

NEVER TOO SMALL

Too small to read the words
And just trying to sing along
A want to just praise the Lord
You know it can't be wrong

To be part of the body
Even though she was only three
Made me thank my God even more
When I began to see

It's not how old you are
Or all the things you know
It's about willingness in spirit
And just wanting to grow

Even though she could not read
To understand the words
She was doing her very best
By repeating what she heard

Now when it got too hard
And she did not know what to do
She went to the Lord herself
With the only song she knew

It doesn't matter how small the seed is
When the Lord wants it to live
He just waters it with living water
As only He can give

Now I hope this opens up your eyes
Because it really did for me
To understand the meaning to the words
To a song called *Jesus Loves Me*

JESUS IS

Who is Jesus
And what does He mean to you
Is Jesus just there to lean on
Or in everything you do

Is He there for the good times
Or only in the bad
And how about the happy
Or only in the sad

Jesus is the Spirit
That wants to live within
It doesn't matter who you are
Or the color of your skin

Jesus is with you always
All you have to do is call
He is there in every season
Winter, spring, summer and fall

Jesus is the breath of life
That we all need to breathe
To keep us all alive
And for this we must believe

Jesus is almighty
How much more can you say
But I will leave that up to you
When you take the time to pray

I SAID, HE SAID

(I Said) What do you want from me
(He Said) It's not just for you
But everyone you see
So tell them the story
Of the Man from Galilee

(I Said) Well how do I do this
(He Said) Take my book
Have a look
And read it well
Take your shoes off
Grab a coffee
And sit down a spell

Take your time
Have an open mind
There's a story to tell
About how to live forever
And beat the man from hell

So take my book and have a look
And beat the man from hell

(I Said) Sounds like a good one
(He Said) Tell of how Jesus walked among them
Each and every day
Healing the sick and teaching how to pray
Tell about what He preached
As He travelled from place to place
About love, joy and peace
Forgiveness, faith and grace

(I Said) Wow
(He Said) Tell of what He gave
Just for you and me
When He died on the cross that day
On a hill at Calvary

Tell people that through His blood
The world was set free
The price was paid in full
For sinners like you and me

(I Said) Forgive me, I am leaving
I have some things to do
(He Said) All is forgiven,
so read the book, tell the story,
You know what to do
(I Said) Thank you

KEYS

I had a set of keys
But I did not know what for
I did not know where they came from
Or that they could open up a door

You see I had the keys to the kingdom
But this was new to me
I did not know how to use them
In order to be free

I had tried many different doors
In my life along the way
But not one of them would open
Until I took the time to pray

I did not know how to ask
At the very start
But Jesus filled in the blanks
And started cleaning out my heart

He knows what you are going to say
Before you even start
Because He loves you deeply
And knows what's in your heart

Now one of these keys is called the Lord's prayer
And it helps you enter in
To a personal relationship with Jesus
And you can only win

Another key is called the Helper
Or the Holy Ghost
This is the key the Father sends
To simply be His host

The Helper is like a messenger
Going from place to place
Doing all of God's will
With His amazing grace

He is sent to guide you
When you are gathered in Jesus name
And after you first feel His presence
You will never be the same

Now Jesus is love
And He is the master key
Jesus can open any door
He always sets you free

Now I still have some keys left
That I do not know what for
But I tell you what I am going to do
And that's pray a whole lot more

STINKY

I used to stink
And smell real bad
So I went to the doctor
To find out what I had

He said I can't help you
You are not the only one
This always happens
When you forget the Father's Son

The One who made you
From the very start
And let me tell you people
It nearly broke my heart

You see a long time ago
When I entered in
I got killed with the law
I guess you call it sin

It had really hurt me
And a lot of others too
Is it not amazing
What good people do

So I started praying
To the Lord up above
And an answer came back
And it was filled with love

Jesus said He was looking for me
That He loved me and always will
And if I did not know by now
That He had paid my bill

He said if your cup is empty
You can drink from Mine
And you don't need to worry
All will be just fine

I said dear Lord I am sorry
For I am filled up with shame
And I did not want to hurt
Your holy, holy name

Jesus said use My Name
In everything you do
And with all of My authority
For I have given it to you

SO CALLED FRIENDS

My walk was very slow
And my light was very dim
You see my heart was not clean at all
And it was filled with sin

I used to drink and do drugs
And mostly was quite loud
For I thought I was cool
And of this I was so proud

You see I thought I was happy
Just happy being bad
But I was not happy at all
Just hurt and very sad

Now when I sit and look back
At all the things I've done
And all of my so called friends
Each and every one

If I could go back to
Each one and simply say
Jesus loves you very much
And He is the better way

To let them know Jesus is the drug
And the drink that is so strong
And when you wake up the next day
He is still there not empty or all gone

To tell them they are not the only ones
And they will not be the last
To give their heart to Jesus Christ
And let go of their past

We all have done things
Of which we are not proud
But learn to talk to Jesus
And learn to talk out loud

To confess Him before others
And share that holy name
And pretty soon your light won't be dim
You will be carrying a flame

SOME PEOPLE

Some are here to deliver the message
And others to receive
But in order for this to happen
We all must believe

So open up your hearts
And look deep within
And fill up on Jesus
For you can only win

Talk to the One
The One who is Most High
Tell Him the truth about everything
And watch your troubles go bye-bye

To sit in fellowship
Is an honour to me
To be thankful and praise His name
That's where we need to be

Now let's make it personal
Between the Lord and you
Just ask for it in prayer
And see what He will do

FREE

Now sometimes when I write
I will just sit and cry
When I think about my Lord and Saviour
And why He had to die

And all that Jesus gave up
Not just for you and me
But to do His father's will
And set the world free

Free to worship
And praise Jesus holy name
And simply ask forgiveness
For this is why He came

Free from all the things
That can only hold you back
So let's give Jesus all the glory
And try to stay on track

Sometimes we need to see things
In a different light
Sometimes we need to do things
That we know are right

So ask not what Jesus can do for you
But what you can do for Him
Because when you are a servant
He simply lives within

SIGNS AND WONDERS

Unless we see signs and wonders
That is what Jesus said
I mean just watch TV
Or read a newspaper instead

They are everywhere
If you take the time to look
In something called the Bible
It's much more than a book

Just take the time to read it
It's supposed to be your sword
To fight off unwillingness
That keeps us from the Lord

Some signs we read everyday
But they don't sink into our mind
And wonders they are everywhere
Just seek and you shall find

Signs and wonders
Were given as a warning
So ask Jesus into your heart
And wake up with Him each morning

Pray to God that you are worthy
And can stand up to the test
And simply try to be yourself
That's who you are the best

Knock on that Jesus door
And it will be opened just for you
And when you see signs and wonders
You will know what to do

MOUNTAIN CLIMBING

Times have been hard and slow
I have been going through a valley
Every time I tried to get on track
I got beat up in the alley

Sometimes I wonder how
I ever make it out
It can only be Jesus
Of this there is no doubt

Jesus is always there
To catch us when we fall
To help stand us up again
We just need to call

Sometimes when things are good
We seem to lose our way
Jesus is still there
But we forget to pray

So when you are in a valley
And you just need a friend
Just leave it up to Jesus
He's the beginning and the end

So take the time to pray
And simply say thank you
Because mountain climbing is hard work
And it is easier with two

TEARS

Have you ever cried out of thankfulness
Because of something someone else has done
Being so grateful it touched your heart
And the tears began to run

I thought about my Lord and Saviour
And all He has done for me
He just does it from His heart
It comes so naturally

Who else do you know
That could only be that kind
I've thought and thought
But no one comes to mind

So I am going to tell you something
I am sure you've heard before
But please stop and take some time
To decide and make for sure

Are you ready to give up
And let the Lord have His way
Because when you start it gets harder
Not easier like some people say

No one said it would be easy
But the Lord will help you through
You just need to trust in Jesus
In everything you do

It's hard to give up the old
And believe something new
But all Jesus wants to have
Is a relationship with you

So if you end up crying
And tears come running down
This is a normal process
For tearing Satan's kingdom down

The Lord is listening
When you are crying out to Him
Just say what's on your heart
Let it come from deep within

There is something about tears
They don't even make a sound
But the Lord sees every one
And knows what brought them down

He knows when your heart is true
And you mean what you say in prayer
So just take it to the Lord
And let Him meet you there

TOGETHER IN HIM

Let's all be friends
And praise Jesus together
No matter the race or language
We only can get better

For together we are strong
The strongest of all
But if we are divided
Divided we will fall

Alone we get tired and run down
And simply played right out
But with you and me and Jesus
There is never any doubt

Jesus is always there
To help along the way
To give us hope and build us up
As we live from day to day

There is strength in numbers
That is what people say
So how powerful are we
When we all take time to pray

So let us all be friends together
In this lifetime and the next
Because Jesus is the beginning and the end
And that's what I like best

SOMEDAY WHEN

Someday when you are a grandparent
Maybe you will understand
How it feels to reach down
And take your grandchild by the hand

Sometimes it only gets better
When she is looking up at me
With her arms stretched out
Just wanting and simply needing me

Just a little comforting
From someone that she trusts
Kind of like it is with God
And Him watching over us

What a kind and loving Father
To His children everyone
When you are kneeling at His feet
Asking through the Son

In the name of Jesus
For there is no other door
And once you have knocked on it
You will be going back for more

For the strongest thing in life
That you will ever do
Is when you're on your knees in prayer
Just the Lord and you

LIFE SENTENCE

I was given a life sentence
Just the other day
Funny how this happens
When we forget to pray

Satan stood up proud as can be
Reading out all the charges
There were many
And they were all for me

He brought up all the bad things
That I thought were in my past
And I mean he had every one
From the very first to the last

He said do you have a lawyer
And that he could not help me anyway
He said I was headed straight for hell
And hell is where I would stay

I said Jesus is my lawyer
For Jesus knows all I have done
And I asked Him for forgiveness
Because He is the Father's Son

Satan shook and trembled
And said that is not enough
That he would drag my name through the mud
And that he was big and tough

I told Him about Calvary
And the power of the blood
And that Jesus washed me clean again
All because of love

Now when I looked up
Satan had simply gone away
Satan knew he had no power there
When I took time to pray

Now my life sentence
Did not send me off to jail
It was quite the opposite
For Jesus paid my bail

So when court was over
I thanked Jesus for all He had done
He said remember My commandment
For there is only one

To love as He loved
There is no greater love than this
So I said thank you once again
And Jesus said court has been dismissed

ONE DAY

One day I told the devil
You can never win
I gave my heart to Jesus
And if you don't like it
Take it up with Him

The One most powerful
Who knows everything from first to last
The One with all the answers
To every question asked

Because He is my future
And all there is to be
And Jesus has something you don't have
And that's love
And that's all there needs to be

I have been reading a book
In case you have not heard
It is called the Holy Bible
And it's the living Word

So when the evil one
Comes to call again
Just tell Him Jesus lives in your heart
And with Him you will remain

MY JOURNEY

My journey with the Lord
Started out kind of slow
But as seasons changed and I got older
It began to grow

Little by little
The more I let Jesus in
The more I asked forgiveness
The less there was of sin

You see Jesus opened up a door
And really made me free
I don't know why it took so long
Could it have just been me

Sometimes we hold ourselves back
In everything we do
Because the hardest one to forgive
Is nearly always you

So forgive, set free
And go about your day
And when it starts to build up again
Don't forget to pray

You see, sometimes a journey
Can be slow or very fast
The answer is forgiveness
So let go of your past

COME IN (HOLY SPIRIT)

Come in, build a fire
Warm yourself, let it grow
And take the warmth of the Lord
Wherever you may go

Let His warmth flow through you
So it can comfort others too
Share the fire that was built
Between Jesus Christ and you

Let it spread through out the world
For that is why Jesus came
So a spark that started long ago
Could become eternal flame

A fire that was made
Just to purify
Just like with gold or silver
But it is you and I

A fire so strong and true
It will never be put out
One that lives deep inside your heart
For that is what it's all about

So go and tell all people
The things that you have heard
Because the fuel for this fire
Is the preaching of the Word

A HOUSE

A house is just a house
When it is standing all alone
But when you let Jesus in
A house becomes a home

A place to live in love
That's what Jesus wants for you
A place to live in peace
In everything we do

A home that is filled with joy
Just simply all the time
A place to praise and worship
And spend some holy time

A place to share the word
And lift up Jesus' name
A place to teach your children
Why our Saviour came

A place to laugh and cry
As a family does together
And to grow as one in God
For nothing could be better

Jesus can make a home
Deep inside your heart
You just need to let Him in
And He will never part

L J P F F G

If you are feeling down and out
Just find a special place
And simply repeat the words
Love, Joy, Peace, Forgiveness, Faith and Grace

You see Love is all you can give
And without it not a soul can live

And Joy, well it's a whole lot of fun
And without it life would be so glum

And Peace is a very pleasant spirit
And if you get real close you can even hear it

Forgiveness is for all to have
From the first to the last
It sets us free, you and me
From everything in past

Then there is Faith
The one you need the most of all
It helps us in our daily walk
To stand up straight and tall

And then we end with Grace
A very special word
It means were under God's protection
In case you have not heard

So put them all together
Love, Joy, Peace, Forgiveness, Faith and Grace
And you will find yourself with Jesus
In a very special place

OVERFLOW

I woke up this morning
And it seems we had some rain
To soften up the ground
And help things grow again

Kind of like most people
We can get a little dry
Without Jesus the living water
Most assuredly we would die

Jesus said if your cup is empty
You can drink from mine
You will never thirst again
And all will be just fine

We are all Jesus' fountains
Waiting to overflow
Filling people with the Word
And helping them to grow

So think of yourself as living water
As you go about your day
And when you want to overflow
Just take the time to pray

So simply just take everything
To the Lord in prayer
There is nothing to big or small
Jesus will be there

THE MAN I WAS

Now I am not the man
That I simply was before
Since I met my Lord and Saviour
Now this I know for sure

The Lord has simply changed me
A little at a time
Forgiving and loving me
My God is very kind

Jesus knows all we have been through
All that is and ever will be
Jesus is that guiding light
There for you and me

A light that always shines
So very strong and true
And nothing can compare
To what Jesus Christ will do

He has forgiven you and me
Simply forgotten all our past
What a kind and loving God
Who will always last

Last all through time
Like the Bible says He will
Giving hope to all who call on Him
For Jesus paid our bill

Now I am so glad to say
I am not the man I used to be
Since I let Jesus in my heart
There have been big changes in me

Changes for the better
The answer to some prayers
Done by someone else
Who took the time to care

To care about others
Just like Jesus said to do
There is no greater love than this
And its unconditional too

No strings attached
Just a blessing to receive
From our Lord and Saviour
As long as we believe

Believe it will happen
And simply will come true
For there is really nothing
That Jesus cannot do

Now I have to thank Him
For all the changes in me
Once just a lost man
But now Jesus lives in me

So please just kneel down
And give Jesus Christ your heart
Let Him have some room to work
And He will never part

LOVE YOUR NEIGHBOUR

Jesus, Jesus, Jesus
Gave these words to me
Love your neighbour as yourself
And set the captive free

We all get held captive
In many different ways
Some because of things we do
Or maybe what we say

In order to love your neighbour
You have to learn to love yourself
So give it all to Jesus
His middle name is help

Help when you don't want it
When we are too proud to ask
Or maybe something happened
Way back in our past

For Jesus has seen it all
He is the beginning and the end
Jesus just wants to love you
And simply call you friend

A friend that is forever
There's not to many like that
So just give it all to Jesus
And tell Him where you're at

NO LONGER MINE

I gave my heart to the Lord
Now it's no longer mine
I could not get it to work right anyway
It was broken all the time

I kept getting beat up
Everyday a little more
Things were hurting deep inside
But closed behind a door

A door that never opened out
It only let things in
All of them unworthy
I guess you would call it sin

Now I did not know
When I gave the Lord my heart
That this door had to open up
In order for the healing to start

Slowly but surely
Jesus is doing His work
And when I give up my own will
It don't even hurt

So when you give your heart to the Lord
It's no longer yours
And when there is cleaning up to do
He opens all the doors

So don't try to lock them
The Lord has all the keys
Just cry out to Him in prayer
Down on bended knees

LIGHT UP YOUR DAY

We are all brothers and sisters
In our Lord Jesus Christ
Where there is darkness
He will always give you light

A light so strong and powerful
That it can never be put out
A light that shines for evermore
Of this there is no doubt

Jesus can brighten up
The most dull and dreary day
All we have to do
Is take the time to pray

Pray about anything and everything
Just leave it in Jesus' hands
And learn to be obedient
When making all your plans

Jesus is there to guide us
In everything we do
All we have to do is ask
It's up to me and you

We all have a choice to make
And it is an easy one
For you never can go wrong
With the Father, Spirit, Son

HAVE YOU

Have you ever wrote until
Your pen ran out of ink
Wrote so long and effortlessly
You did not have to think

The words were simply given
For you to write them down
It can only be Jesus, people
Simply all around

It can be hard to write
When your own will is strong
But when you say what Jesus wants
It don't take very long

Jesus loves us all
In His own amazing way
And we take this for granted
This I have to say

We need to honour Jesus
Just as much as we can
Simple praise and worship
I think you understand

Jesus gave us all He could
His very life you see
He just did His Father's will
To set the world free

JESUS NEVER DOES

All may change in life
But Jesus never does
He is the same as yesterday
Could it just be us

Jesus gave us all a choice
With a little thing called free will
It's our choice to make
But Jesus paid our bill

Our bill was paid in full
Many years ago
But this is surely something
Satan don't want you to know

Jesus died for everyone
And rose up from the grave
He gave us all eternal life
He simply came to save

To save all the people
The Gentile and the Jew
There's no discrimination in the Lord
In what He came to do

Now some are caught up in the world
And others in the law
Sometimes I think we leave our Father
Just sitting there in awe

In awe of what we will do
And think it's still o.k.
We need to ask forgiveness
And simply turn away

Turn away from things we are doing
Wrong from the very start
We need to listen to the Lord
And let Him in our heart

Repent and forgive
Two words that stand alone
For we can only live
If we use these in our home

To live a life worth living
Every single day
Just leave it up to Jesus
For He will show the way

Jesus knows the road
We are never all alone
Jesus walked it long before us
When the earth was His home

SAILING SEAS

We are all God's vessels
Sailing on the open seas
And we become a major fleet
Down on bended knees

As a fleet we are strong
Working all together
Helping and guiding one another
Through all kinds of weather

When we take Jesus with us
In all we do from day to day
Nothing can come against us
When we take the time to pray

So pull your sails up high
To the top of your mast
And sail around with freedom
For Jesus has got your back

Jesus wants His vessels
As clean as they can be
So think about what you do
And pray for it, you see

Jesus wants to use you
To help do His will
And when your vessel's clean and empty
You are there to fill

To fill with all the gifts
That Jesus has in store
A blessing everyone
He wants to give you more

HEARTS, SOULS, MINDS

Jesus is the washboard
Before things hit the line
Jesus does not do clothes
But hearts, souls, and minds

Jesus will clean you up
Just as shinny as can be
Jesus knows just what is needed
In order to set you free

Free from all the things
That simply get in our way
And separate us from God
That's why we have to pray

We all get dirty
In many different ways
Things seem to attach themselves
That only Jesus can take away

Jesus is the one
Who can make you shinny clean
Jesus is the answer
To every single dream

For Jesus can make them happen
I know He has done this for me
I still get dirty now and then
But He cleans me up, you see

I just go back on the washboard
And hang out on the line
And let Jesus have His way
With my heart, my soul, my mind

MORE EXTREME

Everyone wants it new
Or maybe more extreme
It never seems to be enough
Do you understand what I mean

It has to be more intense
Or maybe to the max
Were we like that when we were young
And should we just relax

It seems there have been changes
Right from the beginning of time
So why don't we understand
This concept in our mind

Some people don't care at all
And others say what's the fuss
And then I have to tell them
What Jesus done for us

If you want extreme
Go and part the sea
I don't know about you
But it did not work for me

And let's take it up a notch
And even to the max
When Jesus died on the cross that day
And covered all our backs

Now sometimes I think
We got it all to good
We just turn up the thermostat
Instead of chopping wood

We don't have to feed the animals
Or do any chores
Everything is on remote control
Even the opening of doors

Now it seems to me
I can get stuck in the past
But let's all slow down a little
We are going way to fast

We need to remember what was given
And what was lost
It's about what was sacrificed
And the life that it cost

We need to honour Jesus the Christ
And give praise to His Holy name
And be thankful and humble
That Jesus never changed

Just to give glory
To the One who is Most High
And never, ever, ever forget
Why Jesus had to die

BEST FRIENDS (THANKS)

High on a mountain
That's where I want to be
Me and my best friend Jesus
Looking after me

To glorify His Holy name
In each and every way
And to say dear friend thanks a lot
For teaching me to pray

For teaching me to rise up
In Your Mighty name
And simply tell all people
That life is not a game

For teaching me to be humble
And to take the time to think
That You're the living water
And of You I am to drink

For teaching me to hear
And listen for your call
Can't you hear Him, people
He is talking to us all

And for teaching us to love
For that's what we are to do
And if we only do that much
We will have a best friend too

NEVER BUSY

Who do you give it to
And just what do you say
When you have no place to turn
And it is simply a bad day

The Lord is always there
All you have to do is call
The line is never busy
And there is no charge at all

All you have to do
Is give up a little time
And give Jesus all the burdens
Of your heart, your soul, your mind

Jesus has a way with things
That's heavenly and wise
We have no way to understand
And no need to question why

We just need to love Him
That's what He does for you and me
A shelter for us all
That sets the captive free

To give Jesus the glory
For all that He has done
All He is going to do
And all that is to come

Just to give the credit
Where it is really due
And be thankful most of all
God gave up His Son for me and you

TO FAST

With all of today's technology
The beast is very different today
It's the same old devil doing things
Just coming out in a different way

People are never happy
They just want more than before
There are still only 24 hours in a day
But we keep trying to make more

We need to slow down
Be still and listen to the Holy Spirit
But at the speed we are all going
We take no time to hear it

We need to unplug from e-mail
Voice mail and the cell phone
And shut off our computers
And give Jesus back our home

We rush, rush, rush
No matter what we do
There is never enough time
For what we have to do

So if we all slow down and think
And there is still too much to do
Try not to do it all in one day
Maybe it should be done in two

Take the time to think
(I know that's a lot of Ts)
And something else that helps a lot
Is prayer on bended knees

You can burn the candle from both ends
Only for so long
And one day when you wake up
The middle is all gone

Kind of like our own lives
We start out young and strong
And day by day as we get older
The time is simply gone

So please humble yourself in prayer
It's a small price to pay
For all the Lord has given us
And the help along the way

TWO-YEAR-OLD TEACHER

Humbled by a two-year-old
Going for a walk
I was teaching of the world
When we had to stop

My little granddaughter
Started singing a song
Just a little tiny voice
But it was very strong

Strong in Jesus
For everyone to see
The name of the song she sang
Was *Jesus Loves Me*

Strong in the very meaning
The meaning of the word
I wish you could have been there
So that you could have heard

How a little girl
Just walking down the street
Was singing praise to Jesus
And looking at her feet

Now every step she took
She just sang a little more
And as time would have it
We got back to our door

This is something that really
Just happened one day
And I thank Jesus for two-year-olds
That sing along the way

These were precious moments
For a grandfather to see
Because a seed that was planted
Sprouted right in front of me

So sometimes we need to listen
For the smallest voices heard
Because two-year-olds can be messengers
In the preaching of the Word

BODY PARTS

Something happens to me
When I start to write things down
It's like there's a message there
Just waiting to be found

To be shared with everyone
For that is what the Lord had said
To me when this all started
Filling up in my head

Just to share His word
Is a great honour to me
And it gets even better
When you are in the body

Many people all together
Praying in the spirit
Knowing that the Lord is there
And that He will hear it

To know that we are all different
And still very much the same
And the power we have as one
In Jesus' Holy name

So let's all be body parts
In Jesus for the same cause
Because when we are in agreement
We don't have any flaws

To do His will as one
Is what Jesus wants for all
So think about what you just heard
And listen for His call

JESUS TIME

I got up one morning
It was about 6:30
I knew it was Jesus time
Because I don't get up that early

I did not know what Jesus wanted
Or what I was to do
So I sat down with my coffee
And started writing this for you

He said it's a new day
And it's starting out just fine
I am glad you heard Me calling
And simply took the time

To get up with me
And take your pen in hand
And do My will not yours
I think you understand

Understand I just love you
Always have and always will
You see that's why I died
So I could pay your bill

We all need to take the time
To simply hear His call
You might have to get up early
But Jesus is for all

And don't forget to say I love you
And thank you very much
Praise and glory be to you Lord
For You have given, oh so much

LOOKING FOR SOMETHING

I was looking for something
For a long, long time
And it was right at home
It was just a book you see
Sitting on a self
But it was all alone

So I picked it up and opened it
And it did the same for me
The more I read with willing eyes
The more it set me free

Now a book is just a book
Until you open up its cover
But this book was called the Bible
And the Lord I would discover

I did not know what He wanted
Or what really was in store
All I know is the more I read
The more I wanted more

A lot more of everything
That was coming from within
Like love and joy and peace
And the forgiveness of sin

I met a man named Jesus
Who simply said to me
You must be born again
So come and follow me

I will simply show you more
As you keep reading on
And I will send the Holy Spirit
To help when I am gone

I will never leave or forsake you
For this is written in the Word
So go and preach the gospel
And tell of what you heard

ONE MORNING

I got up one morning
And it was kind of early
I did not know why at first
But I was in a hurry

I put some water in the pot
And threw the coffee in
And as I thought to myself
I began to grin

You see the night before
When I went to bed
I said some simple prayers
And then laid down my head

I said the Lord's prayer
For that's how I always start
Then I ask for forgiveness
To clean up my heart

I prayed for my family
Neighbours and friends
And I prayed for all my enemies
But that is not where it ends

I prayed for every house in the world
That they would have love, joy and peace
And Jesus watching over them
Just like me, then I went to sleep

You see it is morning now
And night time is all gone
So I need to pray again
To keep me from all wrong

LIVE IT

It seems to me you must live it
If you are going to write it down
But in my case I must give it
At least that is what I found

Some very fine things
Have been laid upon my table
And I must tell you about them
As long as I am able

The Holy Spirit came to me
And gave a little touch
And I have been trying to live it
But it seems there is too much

He told me from the very start
That it was not just for me
That I would have to share it
And that's the way that it should be

The Lord said to love as He loved
That there is no greater love than this
And if we this all our lives
Nothing will have been missed

I cannot say it has been easy
Writing all the time
But this is my gift to you
Because writing has become mine

(EMPTY) LIVING WATER

There I was on empty
Driving down the road
Carrying all my burdens
Such a heavy load

So I stopped to talk to Jesus
And empty out my heart
To simply say I am sorry
For keeping us apart

To let Him know I love Him
Each and everyday
And to remind myself
To take the time to pray

So when your cup gets empty
And really need a drink
Go to the well of living water (Jesus)
Instead of the kitchen sink

OUR FATHER

We all start out as babies
In our father's eyes
He holds us close and loves us lots
This comes as no surprise

As we all grow bigger
He slowly lets us go
In the hope that we will find
What we need to grow

Some grow very slowly
And others very fast
For these are precious moments
They never seem to last

And before you know it
They are just as big as you
You want to hold them close and love them lots
Just like you used to do

LAZY ME

I guess I was just lazy
When I entered in
I wanted everything
Without losing sin

But there were some things
I had to conquer first
And when I found out what they were
I mean, they were the worst

I had to swallow up my pride
And throw it all away
And clean up my heart
Each and every day

You see Jesus is a doctor
With the perfect pill
But in order to eat it
You must give up your will

And when these things came to pass
And finally were all done
I went back to the Doctor
To tell of what I had done

He said you're set free
And all is forgiven
So take My pill and do My will
And stop that lazy livin'

I LET JESUS IN

One day I let Jesus in
Now I cannot get Him out
It seems He is here to stay
Of this there is no doubt

Jesus came in
So hard and so fast
He hit me with forgiveness
Now I forgot my past

Now I was hoping that
Jesus would just slow down
I mean it nearly killed me
This new thing that I found

I guess I did not find Jesus
He was looking for me
And when it comes to search and rescue
He is the best you see

Let me tell you folks
I tried to get away
But Jesus would have none of that
With Him I am to stay

So I finally just gave up
It was easier you see
I am not getting any younger
And sin is killing me

So when Jesus makes up His mind
That's the way it is going to be
Don't try to get Him out
It never worked for me

THE BOOK

I started reading a book
That I have not finished yet
And Lord knows it's a good one
It's all about life and death

The life it gives you
From the very start
Even before you are born
There is beating in your heart

Just a little sign
From Him up above
About how precious life really is
And a little thing called love

Now as far as death goes
We can't stop it if we try
We don't know when it will happen
But we always question why

Why did God let this happen
We put the blame on Him
And then I go to the part in this book
On something we call sin

The wages of sin are death
And we will all collect our pay
But I hope I am done reading
Before I pass away

Now I have left out
Many parts it seems
But you will have to read it
To find out what it means

My book is called the Bible
I guess I forgot to say
And it takes a lifetime to read it
Not just a single day

DYING NOT SO BAD

I am happy to say I am dying
A little more each day
The closer I get to Jesus
The old me fades away

No more I, I, I, me, me, me
There is just Jesus and love
And that's the way it's supposed to be

Sometimes it's hard
For the old me to die
And when I am writing what He said
It will even make me cry

To think I have been blessed
By the One who is Most High
Makes it an honour and a privilege
Even when I die

So die a little bit
It really is o.k.
Because Jesus loves you very much
And that's all there is to say

FREE INDEED

What do people really want in life
When you really stop and think
How much garbage can you have
Before it starts to stink

Sometimes it is in the house
Could be in the shed
It may be in the yard
Or underneath the bed

Things get piled up everywhere
And sometimes in our heart
We should have cleaned it out long ago
Way back at the start

It would have been easy then
If we could have let it go
Instead we are still hanging on
And it's got nowhere to go

We need to give it to Jesus
And lay it at His feet
And ask for forgiveness
And, if necessary, repeat

When you wash it in the blood
And you hang it on the cross
It's not like the landfill
And there is not any cost

It says in John chapter 8 and verse 36
If you take the time to read
Therefore if the Son makes you free
You shall be free indeed

HUMBLED IN SPIRIT

Sometimes to be humbled
Is the best medicine of all
It gives us time to think
And hear our Master's call

To look at things in a different light
That we did not see before
Because we were stuck in darkness
And light opens up that door

By the grace of God we are saved
And I humbly say thank you
Because through God's grace
We receive His mercy too

So when you get humbled
If you really stop and think
The Lord is just weeding what was planted
And then giving it a drink

A drink of that living water
The one so sweet and pure
The one we need every day
So that we can endure

Let me say I have been humbled
Just writing this down for you
Praise and glory to our Lord
And most of all thank you

CUTTING CORNERS

Everyone is cutting corners
Way to much I have found
There is nothing square no more
Everything is turning round

Now where does it stop
And just where will it end
There are no limits anymore
To the rules that we can bend

When will people stand up
And fight in Jesus name
And take back what was given
When our Saviour took the blame

We don't stop at signs
Or go home to use the phone
We don't have supper as a family
We mostly eat alone

When we wash our hair
The shampoo is 2-in-1
There is no time for cream rinse
And we dry it on the run

We need to slow down
And remember why we are here
For the Lord is coming back
The Bible makes this clear

So please stop cutting corners
And take the time to pray
Jesus loves to hear you call
And help you along the way

WELCOME

Come on in Lord
And make yourself at home
All of this is really yours
Should the truth be really known

There is nothing in this world
That I can hold back from You
When I give up my own will
And do as you would have me do

Lord let me learn to trust in You
Just like You trust in me
When You say I am forgiven
And see only good in me

Give me the strength each day
To keep reaching out to You
You are my Lord and Saviour
So holy and so true

Thank you for the Spirit
That lives deep inside of me
Thank you for the blood You shed
Nailed upon a tree

Lord You are welcome
So do with me what You will
Chasten me as a Father would
And I will love You still

A HUMBLE GARMENT

Little time is left
And there are lots of things to do
Like lifting up Jesus' name
In everything we do

We need to put on the garment of humility
So we do not stumble
For God resists the proud
But gives grace to the humble

We are to submit to God
By doing all His will
Standing steadfast in our faith
Waiting and being still

So we can hear the Lord
And what He wants to say
Let's all get in the Spirit
And let Him show us the way

Some things we must suffer
Knowing we are not alone
The Lord is always with us
Waiting to take us home

We need to look in 1st Peter
Start at chapter 3 and verse 8
We are called to inherit a blessing
But time is getting late

So please, please read on
You do not have to stop there
There is lots of spiritual food for all
The Lord wants to share

THREE WORDS

Lord I took my pen in hand
To say what You mean to me
I thought and thought about the words
And could only come up with three

Now the first word is *hope*
Without it we would all be lost
It puts us with the Lord one day
And reminds us of the cost

It also gives us character
So we can persevere
That through our Lord and Saviour
We can overcome all fear

Then there is *faith*
I don't know a stronger word
It's all about believing
Through the preaching of the Word

Faith is the substance of things hoped for
The evidence of things not seen
Look in Hebrews chapter 11 verse 1
To find out what I mean

So it seems we need *hope* and *faith*
And they work really well together
And when you add *love* in there
Nothing could be better

Now *love* is a word
That does not stand alone
It's there with many others
And wants to fill up every home

Jesus said to love as He loved
Greater love has no one than this
And if we do this all our lives
Nothing will have been missed

If you read in 1st Corinthians
Starting in chapter 13 and verse 1
And just keep on reading there
Until the whole chapter is done

Hope and *faith* and *love*
Have been given to you and me
We just need to use them
In order to be free

So I pray you got the message
That three words can give
And use them in your daily walk
As long as you shall live

SLOW AND STEADY

I woke up one morning
And sure enough the old me was dead
The Lord had simply answered
The prayers that I had said

I had asked blessings for my neighbours
My family, relatives and friends
The poor, the sick, the needy
But that's not where it ends

I prayed for all my enemies
That they could know Jesus too
And then I said dear Lord please
Take out of me what is not of you

I had prayed this many times
This is something you need to know
But I did not know when it started
That many things must go

But slow and steady
The Lord's work is being done
All those things that had to go
Are leaving one by one

And the more I pray
And simply ask of my Father
The more He encourages me
And tells me it's no bother

He said that's what I am here for
In case you did not know
I pull out all the weeds
So My little ones can grow

Now please don't think I am being mean
When I pray you wake up dead
For you are never more alive
When you're the answer to prayers said

EASTER

Now what can we say about Easter
It simply stands alone
Nothing greater was ever done
Than our Saviour going home

The One who gave up everything
Just to do His Father's will
Knowing all it would cost Him
But yet Jesus did it still

Not thinking about Himself
But everyone you see
Jesus laid down His life
Just for you and me

He gave us all a cup to drink from
That never will run dry
Jesus made a way to the Father
That's why He had to die

Now Easter is not about rabbits
Or chocolate covered eggs
Or any other idols
That man has ever made

They put a sign above the cross
That said the King of the Jews
But when Jesus died
He made way for Gentiles too

For anyone who would believe
And simply call on His name
There is no discrimination in Christ
For we are all the same

So let's all try to remember
What Jesus came to bring
It's about everlasting life
Praise and glory to our King

PLEASE LET ME TELL YOU HOW

Please let me tell you something
Right here and right now
If you don't know Jesus
Please let me tell you how

Please get down on your knees
And say what's on your heart
Just tell the Lord the truth
Then a relationship can start

You will need to do some reading
Like John chapter 3 and verse 16
And then go to Romans chapter 10 verse 9
And you will find out what I mean

Then go to Romans chapter 3 verse 23
We are all with you there
We all fall short of the glory of God
We need the sinner's prayer

And maybe after that
You will start to understand
It's not about you and me
It's time to make a stand

You see Jesus loves us all
No matter what we have done
We just need to call on Him
To put Satan on the run

Take a look at James chapter 4 verse 6
It will tell you what to do
Put your faith in God Almighty
And He will be there with you

Then go back to the book of John
To chapter 13 and verse 34
There is a new commandment there
And see what it is for

Now these are given scriptures
For all to receive
The good news that they bring
To help us all believe

So he who has an ear
Please Lord let them hear it
So they can come to know You too
And be filled with Your Spirit

IT ONLY GETS STRONGER

I was praying to my Father
Just talking like a son
Telling of my burdens
Each and every one

Praying for my children
Where ever they may be
Knowing the Lord is there
Just like He is with me

I laughed to myself
When a thought come to my mind
I am a father like my Father
Just so far behind

Behind in our relationship
That should be getting stronger every day
Because I don't always take the time
Just to sit and pray

For me and my Father
Need a lot of one on one
And prayer is the only way
That I can get this done

Knowing my Father loves me
Means the most of all
Knowing He is always there
I just need to call

Seems when you are a father
There are things you must do
To let your children know you're there
When they need someone too

To let them know you love them
Always have and always will
And that's what Jesus did
When He died on a hill

So encourage and give hope
Inspire in all you do
And most of all just love
That's what Jesus said to do

FORGIVE ME

I know I have broken many hearts
In my life I have to say
I pray the Lord will heal them all
And forgive me for my way

I was not thinking of others
Like the Bible tells me to
I was just thinking of myself
And did not have fellowship with you

Only God can do a miracle
As only He can do
All I can do is ask for it
And believe it will come true

Believe my Father will do this
From heaven up above
Through His grace and mercy
And the power of His love

To think that there is no other
Whose name we can call upon
And that He is always there
Just like the coming of the dawn

For when we are weak
The Lord is very strong
Can you see this, people
To Him we must belong

TRUTH

I am little in body
And sometimes in spirit
My voice is so weak and low
I pray that you can hear it

I have been in pain Lord
For a long, long time
Lord my whole body hurts
Along with my mind

It has not been easy
Being who I am
And how does my family feel
When people pick on them

Lord You know my sinful ways
And everything I have done
I humbly ask forgiveness
For each and every one

Put a new song in my heart
And let me sing it for you
Let it be a blessing to others
Your message powerful and true

Let all people know
That they have to learn to love
And may the peace of God be with you all
Shining down from up above

CHANGES

I think we would all make changes
If we could go back and do it again
I guess that's why we have our prayers
And why our Lord and Saviour came

Please let Jesus be the shepherd
And simply follow Him
Jesus leads you by example
And wants to live within

Just give your heart to Jesus
And let Him take you through
On a path that is straight and narrow
And made for me and you

Let us be that shining light
Sitting high upon a hill
There for everyone to see
Because we gave up our will

Lord may we bring life only
And not death to others
Because each one of them
Are our sisters and our brothers

Let us live in love
Just like Jesus said to do
So everyone will see
That we are disciples too

YOU TOUCHED ME

So why dear Lord Jesus
Have You gifted me so much
You sent the Holy Spirit
To give me a little touch

To give me a little man
A little man in You
Such a taste of Your awesome power
I did not know what to do

So I started writing down
Simply what You said
And I am learning to be obedient
When my own will is dead

To put a pen to paper
In Your Holy name
My Lord You touched me deeply
I will never be the same

MIRACLE

Lord I have been sitting at home
Watching the snow coming down
Knowing it can not be sent back
Once it is laying on the ground

It reminds me of Your awesome power
And that You are almighty too
And there is no way to measure
All the things that You can do

That You are forever
And that You always will be
And that You first loved us
And this we have to see

You sent Your Son
To tear down the veil
To set all the world free
And simply pay its bail

Just to give mankind
Still another chance
At eternal life
Far beyond our circumstance

You are a Holy, Holy God
And miracles come from You
And we should all be thankful
And simply worship You

There is none greater
Nor will there ever be
So thank you, thank you, thank you
From all of us to thee

A SONG

I was listening to a song
And I thought how true
If only we could apply it in our lives
There would be nothing more to do

To put our Lord first
In each and every day
To be thankful that He is there
And not be afraid to say

He is Lord before all
So everyone can meet Him too
Just take the time to share the word
That's what we are supposed to do

Give the glory all to Jesus
He is the One who died
Just ask Jesus in your heart
Let Him come live inside

To fill you with the spirit
As only He can do
Let Jesus be your shepherd
A guide in place for you

And most of all
Just pour out your love
To anyone who needs it
Like our Father up above

SPANKING

We are all beginners
In everything we do
Its no different with Jesus
But He wants the best for you

We are like little babies
Just learning how to walk
We fall down lots of times
And we can hardy talk

Jesus is there always
Kind of like mom or dad
And He still loves us
Even when we have been bad

Sometimes He is there for correction
When we don't want to listen up
I know this has happened
When my own pride button got stuck

Jesus has a different way of spanking
You can take it from me
He let me do it all myself
Until I could finally see

Pride is a big mistake
That we can carry around everyday
Or we can put it where it belongs
If we take the time to pray

And after this spanking
That I got to give myself
I could tell Jesus I was sorry
Because my pride was on the shelf

SOME PEOPLE SAY

Some people say
I have a way with words
But it's not me it's Jesus
In case you have not heard

You see writing, to me
Is a gift from up above
Given to me from Jesus
With His amazing love

Now I thank Jesus
Every single day
For helping me to write down
The things He wants to say

I am just meat and bones
When I am standing by myself
Jesus sends the Holy Spirit
To give all kinds of help

To help me in my daily walk
Whatever that will be
Because each day is always different
And sometimes I cannot see

To help other people understand
The new hope I have found
When I say it is Jesus not me
When I am ten feet off the ground

SORRY

Jesus I am sorry
I know its me again
I really need to talk
And I have to take the blame

The blame for things I have done
If only in my mind
You see I have had some thoughts
And they were so unkind

It had to do with others
And how they treated me
But now its in my heart
And so unclean you see

So please dear Lord forgive me
For the thoughts in my head
And please clean out my heart
Before I go to bed

So I can wake up tomorrow
Feeling all brand new
With a clean heart and mind
And live my life for you

So thank you very much
For having this little talk
And thank you very much
For helping with my walk

YOUR SERVANT

Jesus, I say thank you
For you are the only One
For You have filled my life
With simply so much fun

To think of all the good things
That You put in place for me
I mean there are so many
Everyone can see

See that You are kindness
And all that is good
I would like to be Your servant
So please let me, if You would

Let me get up each morning
Just to see what You have in store
And teach me to be obedient
As You love me more and more

So that we can just get closer
Than we were the day before
And look forward to tomorrow
And what it has in store

A door I can knock on
That's open all the time
Because dear Lord I love You
And for You I want to shine

NEED TO TALK

Sometimes people need to talk
To simply get things out
So tell it all to Jesus
He knows how to sort it out

There is never anything
That He really does not know
He loves you very much
And just wants you to grow

To grow up strong with Jesus
And build up your faith
Jesus will always be there
No matter what it takes

To love you and hold you
Even when you cry
When you are down and out
And life is passing by

So please, just talk to Jesus
And tell Him from within
Just knock on that Holy door
And Jesus will let you in

For Jesus has an answer
For every question asked
And most of all Jesus
Forgives things of the past

BEFORE MEETINGS

Sometimes before I go to meetings
I get filled up with fear
It is only Satan
Talking in my ear

Fear is not of God
That is not how He works
He just uses lots of love
To help with all our hurts

Sometimes we can worry
And become quite afraid
But just remember why Jesus came
And the price that He paid

Jesus is full of love
That's all that He can be
Just love, love, love
And man, it sets you free

There is no other feeling
So powerful and strong
When you give your heart to Him
To Jesus you belong

Now when you give your heart to Jesus
You will always be under attack
But that is what prayer is for
Because Jesus has got your back

Index

To order more copies of this book, find books by other Canadian authors, or make inquiries about publishing your own book, contact PageMaster at:

Lorn Johnson

Growing up, not knowing the Lord, I had prayed to Him at different times in life. I did not know I had to be born again to have a relationship with God. Now, after I gave my heart, that relationship did not grow very much because I did not have fellowship with anyone. I did not go to church or to hang out with fellow believers. When I started to have fellowship with others in the Lord, my relationship with God became more clear. The more I searched the word, the more I asked, the more I wanted to know God, the more God showed me how real He is. I pray the words in this book reach out and touch you. I pray they inspire, encourage, bless and bring a smile in the hope that the peace of God which surpasses all understanding guard our hearts and minds through Christ Jesus.